Dear Family,

What's the best way to help your child love reading?

Find good books like this one to share—and read together!

Here are some tips.

- **Take a "picture walk."** Look at all the pictures before you read. Talk about what you see.

- **Take turns.** Read to your child. Ham it up! Use different voices for different characters, and read with feeling! Then listen as your child reads to you, or explains the story in his or her own words.

- **Point out words as you read.** Help your child notice how letters and sounds go together. Point out unusual or difficult words that your child might not know. Talk about those words and what they mean.

- **Ask questions.** Stop to ask questions as you read. For example: "What do you think will happen next?" "How would you feel if that happened to you?"

- **Read every day.** Good stories are worth reading more than once! Read signs, labels, and even cereal boxes with your child. Visit the library to take out more books. And look for other JUST FOR YOU! BOOKS you and your child can share!

The Editors

To my sisters Beryl and Geraldine, my brother Robert,
my niece Catrina, and my mother Henri Mae.
Thank you all!
—GH

To Myron, Marci, and Myron Jr. (aka "Boot").
Thank you for the inspiration.
—ND

Text copyright © 2004 by Gwendolyn Hooks.
Illustrations copyright © 2004 by Nancy Devard.
Produced for Scholastic by COLOR-BRIDGE BOOKS, LLC, Brooklyn, NY
All rights reserved. Published by SCHOLASTIC INC.
JUST FOR YOU! is a trademark of Scholastic Inc.

Library of Congress Cataloging-in-Publication Data

Hooks, Gwendolyn.
    The mystery of the missing dog / by Gwendolyn Hooks ; illustrated by
Nancy Devard.
        p. cm.—(Just for you! Level 1)
    Summary: Alex's search for his missing dog, Jet, leads him to a tea party in
his sister's room.
    ISBN 0-439-56864-1
    [1. Dogs—Fiction. 2. Lost and found possessions—Fiction. 3. Brothers and
    sisters—Fiction. 4. Parties—Fiction.] I. Devard, Nancy, ill.
    II. Title. III. Series.
    PZ7.H76635My 2004
    [E]—dc22   2004004769

10 9 8 7 6 5 4   05 06 07 08
        Printed in the U.S.A. 23 • First Scholastic Printing, April 2004

The Mystery of the Missing Dog

by Gwendolyn Hooks

Illustrated by Nancy Devard

▲▲▲▲▲ JUST FOR YOU!™ ▲▲▲▲▲
▲▲ Level 1 ▲▲

"Here, Jet!" called Alex.
"Let's go to the park."

Jet didn't bark.
He didn't come running.
Where was that dog?

Could Jet be outside?
Alex looked out front.
Jet wasn't there.

Alex looked out back.
Jet wasn't there.

Maybe Jet was in the basement.
Sometimes he liked to sleep
next to the warm dryers.
Alex went downstairs.

"Mr. Gus! Have you seen my dog?"
Alex asked the super.

"Sorry, Alex," said Mr. Gus.
"Not today."

Alex went back upstairs.
There were so many places
a little dog could hide!
Maybe Jet was in the kitchen.

Alex saw Jet's big box
of dog bones.
The box was open.
But Jet wasn't there.

COOKIES

GOOD BOY!

DOG FOOD

DOG BONES

CRUNCHY DOG BISCUITS

Was Jet in the bathroom?
Jet loved bubble baths.

The tub was empty.
Where was Jet?

Alex went to
his sister's room.

"Hi, Alex!" she said.
"Will you play with me?
I have a new doll."

"I don't have time for dolls,"
said Alex. "I have to find Jet."

Alex went into his own room.
Maybe Jet was there.
Alex always tossed his
smelly socks under thc bed.

Jet liked to sleep on the socks.
But Jet wasn't there now.

Alex looked out the window.
"What if Jet is lost?" thought Alex.
"What if he doesn't know how
to get home?"

BARK!
BARK!
BARK!

Alex ran back to his sister's room.
"I heard barking!" said Alex.
"Is Jet under your bed?"

"No! I don't have smelly socks
under my bed," his sister said.

BARK!
    BARK!
        BARK!

"That **is** Jet," said Alex.

"No, it's not!" said his sister.
"This is my new doll!"

Alex looked at the dolls.
One didn't look like the others.
It looked just like Jet!

It was Jet!

"Come on, boy!" said Alex.
"Let's go to the park."

"Don't go!" said Alex's sister.
"We're having a tea party.
Jet wants to stay!"

"No way!" said Alex.

"But Jet has to eat
his cookies," she said.

"Did you say cookies?"
asked Alex.

"We like cookies!
Jet will stay for the tea party.
And I will, too!"

Here are some fun things for you to do.

Jet and YOU!

Alex is happy when he finds Jet.

Pretend that Jet is YOUR dog.

Would you take him to the park?

Would you teach him tricks?

Would you feed him dog bones?

Draw a picture. Show what YOU and Jet would do together.

Why Did She Do It?

Alex's sister knew where Jet was all the time!

Why didn't she tell Alex?

Did she wish that Jet were her dog?

Did she want to play a trick on Alex?

Maybe she just wanted Alex to play with her!

Write a few sentences about Alex's sister.
Tell why YOU think she didn't tell Alex where Jet was.

YOUR Party

Alex's sister has a tea party for her dolls.
Imagine that YOU are having a party.
Who would you want to come?

Draw a picture of YOUR party.
Show everyone who will be there.

TOGETHER TIME

Make some time to share ideas about the story with your young reader! Here are some activities you can try. There are no right or wrong answers!

Talk About It: In real life, brothers and sisters sometimes make things difficult for each other! Ask your child, "How are Alex and his sister like people you know? Do they remind you of anyone in our family?" If you have sisters or brothers, tell your child about what it was like growing up in your family.

Think About It: Point out that in a mystery, one character usually acts like a detective and searches for clues. Jet's barks are clues that lead Alex to solve the mystery of the missing dog! The illustrator has added a clue, too! Look at all the pictures again. Can you two spot a clue on page 14?

Read More: Visit the library to find more surprising stories about pets, such as *Julius* by Angela Johnson, *Pet Show!* by Ezra Jack Keats, and *Go Away, Dog!* by Joan Nodset.

Meet the Author

GWENDOLYN HOOKS says, "I've loved reading mysteries ever since I was a little girl. I decided to write this book after my own pet disappeared. When "Kitty Kat" Hooks snuck outside, my family and I looked everywhere, but we couldn't find him. Three weeks later, Kitty Kat came home! It was a long and sad three weeks for us. When I wrote this story, I made sure Alex didn't have to search too long before he solved his mystery!"

Gwendolyn Hooks taught math before becoming a stay-at-home mom. About ten years ago, she began writing stories. Now she also runs writing workshops for children and educators. She lives in Oklahoma City, Oklahoma, with her husband Edmond, her son Eddy, and her daughter Alison. Her daughter Leslie lives in Texas. Gwen is also the author of *Three's a Crowd*, another book in the JUST FOR YOU! series.

Meet the Artist

NANCY DEVARD says, "I come from a family with two very creative, supportive parents. They bought me real drawing pads and pencils as soon as I showed an interest in drawing. My dad challenged me to copy a portrait of him freehand, without tracing. I loved that challenge, and practiced drawing from then on."

Nancy is a graduate of Temple University and the Pennsylvania Academy of Fine Arts. She worked as a staff artist for Hallmark Cards, creating many images for the Mahogany Cards division, which publishes African-American greeting cards. Nancy has exhibited her work in galleries on the East Coast and in the Midwest. She lives in Kansas City, Missouri. Another book she has illustrated in the JUST FOR YOU! series is *A Mom Like No Other* by Christine Taylor-Butler.